THE SITUATION AND THE DUTY.

SPEECH

OF

WILLIAM H. SEWARD,

AT

AUBURN, N. Y., OCTOBER 31, 1868.

WASHINGTON, D. C.:
PHILP & SOLOMONS.
1868.

THE SITUATION AND THE DUTY.

SPEECH

OF

WILLIAM H. SEWARD,

AT

AUBURN, N. Y., OCTOBER 31, 1868.

WASHINGTON, D. C.:
PHILP & SOLOMONS.
1868.

THE SITUATION AND THE DUTY.

"Secretary SEWARD," says the *Auburn Daily Advertiser* of October 31, 1868, "this afternoon addressed one of the largest audiences ever convened in Corning Hall. The bare announcement yesterday that he was to speak to-day created an intense anxiety in the public mind to hear him, and when the doors of the hall were thrown open at half-past one o'clock, it was immediately filled to overflowing, many hundreds being unable to gain admittance. Secretary SEWARD was introduced by Rev. Dr. HAWLEY."

DR. HAWLEY'S SPEECH.

In the performance of an agreeable duty, fellow-citizens, I was about to extend, on your behalf, a cordial greeting to our distinguished neighbor and personal friend on this occasion. But your prompt and hearty response to his presence once more on this platform, on the eve of a great popular decision, is of deeper significance than any words of welcome. The desire to hear what, from his position, he may counsel at this time is not less earnest and sincere than at other periods of public concern, when he has spoken to his townsmen, and thus to the whole country, and indeed to the whole world. It only remains for me, in interpreting this desire, to say (here the speaker turned to address Mr. SEWARD) that it springs from recollections and associations which can neither be forgotten nor obscured in the ever-varying phases of political action or popular judgment. And that whatever of merited honor or fame may attach to the career of a public servant, it can never cease to be with him a grateful consciousness that he also holds fast the esteem and affection of those who know him best, among whom stands his home, and with whom, when public service ceases, he expects to mingle in the scenes and duties of ordinary life to its destined close.

Mr. SEWARD was received with immense applause, and proceeded to address his audience as follows:

SPEECH OF SECRETARY SEWARD.

MY FRIENDS AND NEIGHBORS: My long absence on political occasions and my present appearance here are proper subjects of inquiry on your part. In explaining both, I may be able to say all that is proper or necessary to be said in this pleasant interview.

Upon the first point, I might well enough plead official occupation. Official obligations necessarily and justly take precedence over those of private citizenship. The public may properly say to its appointed servants, "these ought ye to have done, and not to leave the others undone." Government occupation is increased by civil war, and necessarily increased by returning peace. It increases with ever-increasing population, territory, and commercial and political connections. But, for all this, you are not to suppose, as many assume, that I am purchasing on Government account all the outlying territories in the universe, [laughter and applause,] or indeed proposing to acquire dominion anywhere beyond the magic circle of the Monroe doctrine.

I might plead inadequate strength. I have reason to thank God, indeed, that neither age, nor indulgence, nor casualty, has brought so great decrepitude as persons have sometimes imagined. Nevertheless I certainly have some years, perhaps enough for a place on the retired list; and some wounds, perhaps enough for a pension, if I were in the military or naval service.

Moreover, every opinion or sentiment of mine, that has a bearing upon the present hour, was spoken long ago; spoken, as I thought, in due time; spoken, either concurrently with or in advance of political events. So true is this, that no one has mistaken my abiding attitude, or pretends now to doubt either my official views or my political relations.

Moreover, as it is the duty of deacons to serve, not to lead in the sacrifice, so it has always seemed to me that it is the duty of Secretaries to serve in the administration, and not to lead in popular assemblies. Possibly you may say, however, that a citizen has no right to be a Secretary when a party or an interest desires him for a leader. I answer that deacons are deacons, not by any choice of their own, but because they are chosen by the church; and certainly I am a Secretary, through no ambition of my own for that office, but because the nation has constitutionally required me to be. It would be a poor act of piety on the part of a deacon to refuse to serve because he preferred to sacrifice; and I humbly think it would be a poor act of patriotism in a citizen to refuse to be a Secretary, because he preferred to be a popular leader. Our places, fellow-citizens, are assigned to us, not by ourselves, but under the providence of God by our associates and fellow-men. Our friends here, Mr. James Seymour and Dr. Steele, are living demonstrations that it is better to be a meek and humble, but efficient deacon, than to be schismatic, quarreling with the priest and dividing the sacred congregation. [Laughter and applause.]

The case, however, is now somewhat changed. I am at home for indispensable private business. I find you in an election to constitute a new administration of the Government of the United States. A theory obtained in the early revival of science that an elixir could be compounded, by the use of which the human constitution could be renewed at the end of every hundred years, and so man become immortal. The quadrennial national election of President and Congress in the United States is just such a periodical renewal as this of the national life, whereby the nation in fact becomes immortal.

The casting of my vote in great elections of this sort is equally the exercise of an inestimable privilege and the performance of a high and sacred duty. Mutual explanation of votes is the only means by which mutual confidence can be preserved among citizens, while it saves suffrage itself from profanation, intrigue, and corruption. In an experience of eighty years under the Constitution which makes us a nation, we have renewed the Republic, in the same prescribed way, by twenty national elections. I have voted and explained in the last eleven; these being all of those national elections that have occurred since I came to the franchise. The present election is the twenty-first of the entire series, and my twelfth one. In this election, just as I expressed myself at the time of each preceding one, I feel that this one may be my last.

Every Presidential election necessarily has a real, although an abstract importance. We have here a republican system instead of the monarchical one. An ultimate adoption of this system by all the American nations is necessary for our security. Every new republic established anywhere constitutes a new bulwark of the Republic of the United States. [Applause.]

Our Republican Government has some peculiar devices of local adaptation and equivalent, designed to operate by way of check and balance. Nevertheless, our Constitution has four essential elements, perhaps no more. These elements are, first, the actual choice of the presiding magistrate by the direct vote of the whole people; second, equal suffrage of all citizens in that election; third, equal representation of all constituent communities in the Republic; and, fourth, conditions and periods of power well defined and absolutely fixed. The casting or the withholding of a vote by any citizen inconsiderately actually impairs, although perhaps imperceptibly, the vigor and energy necessary to the continuance of the Republic, just as the casting or the withholding of all the votes of the people inconsiderately would bring it abruptly to an end.

Standing as we do now at the close of the twentieth administration, I can well conceive that the first election was the most important of all, inasmuch as a mistake then committed in the choice of the first President of the United States, or of the first Congress, might have involved the failure of the system at the very beginning. It was just such a mistake that the French people committed in 1848, when they lost their new republic by electing a Bonaparte instead of a Cavaignac. That mistake having been avoided here, the Government promptly went into successful operation. It soon acquired vigor by custom, and continually gained strength from increasing popular reverence and affection. The nation encountered no crisis until 1860. The election of Abraham Lincoln, in 1860, occurred at a time when a sectional faction, with extensive ramifications, had prepared a formidable rebellion.

The election in 1864 was still more critical. Abraham Lincoln, who had been elected in 1860, had been effectually excluded by the rebellion from recognition or acceptance in one-third of the States. It only remained for the still adhering States to reject Lincoln, as President, in 1864, to effect a speedy, if not an immediate, dissolution of the Union. On the other hand, it was reasonably expected that the reaffirmation in 1864 of the choice made in 1860 would so consolidate the loyal and patriotic hopes of the country in support of the administration, as to enable President Lincoln to prosecute the war as no other President could, and to improve returning peace as no other President could, by combining conciliation with decision, until the Constitution should be re-established throughout the whole Union. Within four months after the election of 1864 the strength of the rebellion was effectually broken, and on the 4th of March, 1865, Abraham Lincoln entered upon his second term of the presidency, for the first time, with full possession of the rebel States ; *de facto* as well as *de jure* the recognized and accepted Chief Magistrate of the whole Republic. (Applause.) With him the Congress and the other departments of the Federal Union were equally recognized and accepted.

The duty which devolved upon the Government in the second administration of Abraham Lincoln, was to save the Consititution and the Union from further revolutionary violence, and by just, generous, and judicious measures to bring the distracted and desolated rebel States back to their constitutional relations with the Federal Union.

We have reached at last the end of that second administration, begun by Abraham Lincoln, and we unfortunately find that its great work, as I have described it, remains as yet only incompletely and unsatisfactorily accomplished. Parties now vehemently dispute whether this failure is the fault of one department or of another ; the fault of the President, or the fault of Congress ; the fault of the executive system of reconciliation, or of the congressional system of reconstruction. I do not enter into that dispute. It already belongs to the past. Nevertheless, I am now inclined to think that it was unreasonable to expect the passions and ambitions of thirty-three free States, and thirty millions of free people so recently and terribly convulsed by civil war, to subside in so short a period as four years. It is the highest attribute of the Almighty, which the divine poet has conceived, that He "stilleth the noise of the seas, and the noise of their waves, and the tumult of the people." The storms must be withheld before the seas can come to rest.

Probably such an intense and pervading political agitation as ours could not have been suddenly repressed without overthrowing public liberty itself, as the Napoleons did at the close of two popular French revolutions.

The choice of our two principal magistrates in 1864 was certainly wisely made. We found out at the beginning of the civil war that neither party, and no party alone without co-operation from the other, could save the country. The people who made the choice in 1864 were neither a Republican party nor a Democratic party, but avowedly and heroically a Union people, and union always means an effective combination of kindred forces. The Union people in 1864 followed the rule which has so generally prevailed of dividing the names to be placed on the presidential ticket between competing sections, parties, or interests, giving the greater weight to the larger section or party. With nice judgment, therefore, they chose Abraham Lincoln, a northern Union patriot of Republican antecedents, to be President, and Andrew Johnson, a southern Union patriot of Democratic antecedents, to be Vice President.

Active hostilities, however, had hardly ended before there appeared a portentous conflict of popular ideas and opinions concerning the proper conditions of peace and reconciliation, and these ideas and opinions had relation to the so-called reconstruction of the State governments in the rebel States. Personal ambitions, of course, entered into the controversy. Social ideas and popular ambitions are inherent in all republics, and revolutions stimulate their rapid development. No one form of political idea, no one form of personal ambition that has presented itself in our recent distractions was new. They all sprang up and in turn attained complete, though many of them only temporary, ascendency during the French revolution of 1789, a revolution which, as we all see, gave way after a short while to a military despotism that still survives. We now see that in the insurrection the rebel States became revolutionary States, not merely revolutionary against the United States, but revolutionary within themselves. As such, they have experienced the fortune of all revolutionary States. Each new political idea, and every distinct personal ambition in revolutionary States, demands either a severe constitutional reform, or a change of the existing constitution altogether. The right of the people and their power in such States to make such changes is not only unchallenged, but is also unchecked. It follows, as a consequence, that no constitution which is forged in the white-heat of revolution ever endures.

We have forgotten that this nation went through the revolutionary crisis practically without any constitution at all. There was indeed a Declaration of Independence from Great Britain and from all other nations, and a precious assertion of human rights ; but no constitutional government was established or framed until seven years after the last belligerent had disappeared from the field.

We can all recollect that brilliant constitutions successively came out like fire-beacons in the murky gloom of the French revolution. All those constitutions were based upon some sound political ideas, and all ought to have been compatible with any patriotic ambition. Yet they succeeded each other so rapidly, that when a politician entered the store of a bookseller in Paris, and asked for the constitution of France, he was answered, "We do not deal here in periodical publications." (Laughter.)

Mexico seems at last to have acquired a constitution, but only after forty years of civil wars, culminating in the great calamity which we have so happily escaped—foreign intervention. Although all the South American republics have been independent through a period of forty or fifty years, yet it cannot be certainly said of any one of them that it has yet definitely accepted and adopted a final constitution. Revolutions have continued to overthrow constitutions there as fast as they have been made. It was unwise, then, to expect that the insurgent States, coming out of their flagrant rebellion, and yet allowed by the Federal Constitution to reconstitute their forms of goverment for themselves and by their own proper act, in conformity with the Federal Constitution, could all at once adopt constitutions which should be permanently satisfactory to themselves and to us, in the presence of an entire new condition of society produced by the emancipation of four millions of slaves. What they have wanted was "time." What we have wanted was patience. These two wants seasonably indicated the course of popular wisdom in regard to restoration, reorganization, or reconstruction, by whatever name it may be called.

Reliance, however, was justly placed upon the advantages which Abraham Lincoln had for overcoming these embarrassments. Leaving out of view his peculiar moral and intellectual qualities, Mr. Lincoln possessed a decided advantage, in the fact that he had conducted the Government with approved fidelity and wisdom through the entire course of the civil war. As the people gave their first confidence to Washington, in organizing the Government, upon the ground that he had safely led them through the revolutionary war ; as the people in 1848 gave their confidence to General Taylor, upon the ground that he had safely led them through the greatest peril of the Mexican war ; so the people were expected to give their full confidence to Abraham Lincoln in restoring the Union, because he had led them successfully through the late terrific revolutionary convulsion of the country.

No wise and candid man thought, at that time, either that the war could be ended, or that peace and reconciliation could be effected, under an administration that did not fully enjoy the public confidence upon two cardinal points, namely, first, the justice of the Union cause in the war ; second, the necessity, wisdom, and justice of the abolition of African slavery which the war had effected. [Applause.]

Abraham Lincoln had a still greater advantage. He had been twice chosen by the people themselves to be their President, their civil chief. They were accustomed to his leadership, and they loved him as an accepted impersonation of their own convictions, no matter how varied those convictions might be. They all knew, or believed they knew, him thoroughly. They had committed themselves to his support in advance. His success would be their own success. His failure would be felt and deplored as their own failure. Thus was enlisted in his favor the national pride, the national affection, and the national gratitude. What combinations could have resisted a magistrate thus armed, and aiming only to complete the great and glorious work of saving the Union, which he himself began?

In an unhappy hour Abraham Lincoln fell by the hand of the assassin. That fearful calamity, which was equally beyond human foresight and human control, suddenly and profoundly interfered with our high purposes and patriotic desires. Human nature, around the whole circle of the globe, and especially in its centre here, recoiled and stood aghast before that great crime. The country sank for a moment into sadness and despair of its future, from which it was aroused to seek and search everywhere, in the Government and out of it, in the North and in the South, at home and abroad, for secret authors, agents, and motives for the horrible assassination. While suspicion attached itself by turns to everybody, it justly fastened itself at last upon the rebellion, and demanded new and severer punishment of the rebels, instead of the magnanimous reconciliation which the beloved President of whom it had been bereaved had recommended. Who will say that this sentiment was unnatural? Who shall say that it was even unjust? Revolution has always the same complex machinery. Besides the public machinery which its managers directly employ, there is always a secret assassination-wheel carefully contrived, and ready to come into activity when a crisis is reached. Revolutionists cannot relieve themselves of all responsibility for it by pleading that it was unknown to themselves. Who can say how far this great crime of assassination has been effective in delaying and preventing the desired reconciliation?

It was in the midst of this distraction that Andrew Johnson came to the presidency, not by virtue of two popular elections to that office, like his predecessor, or even of one such election, but by virtue of his constitutional election to be only Vice President. The unfinished work of the lamented Lincoln devolved upon him. The conditions and considerations which were the advantages in his election as Vice President suddenly became disadvantages to him as President. The southern States and the Democratic party were remembered but too unfavorably by the northern anti-slavery victors, in connection with the rebellion, the civil war, and African slavery.

In addressing himself to the holy work of national reconciliation, the new President proceeded with due deliberation and firmness, decision and vigor. He retained all his lamented predecessor's counsellors. He adopted his lamented predecessor's plan of reconciliation, which seemed to him, as it seemed then to the whole country, to be practicable and easy, because it was simple and natural. It consisted simply in opening the easiest and shortest safe way for a return into the national family of the people of the southern States, who now repented their attempted separation. Those States were invited to resume the vacant chairs in the legislative councils, by sending Senators and Representatives, who should be chosen by the people of those States, and who should prove themselves, by every practical test, unquestionably loyal to the Union. Some constitution and frame of government in the rebel States, however, would be a necessary instrumentality of making such choice of Senators and Representatives. There was at the same time a manifest necessity for such renewed institutions of municipal government for the restoration of peace and order in the disorganized States, the administration of justice, and the exercise of other necessary functions of government there. The people of the rebel States were therefore invited to establish such necessary State governments, upon the basis of loyalty and fidelity, of which practical tests were provided. These tests were: first, the acceptance of the new amendment to the Constitution which abolished African slavery; second, repudiation of the rebel debt; third, abrogation of all rebel laws; fourth, the acceptance of the so-called iron-clad oath.

All other questions were passed over for further and future action. Loyal State governments were promptly formed, and loyal Senators and Representatives appeared with equal promptness at the doors of Congress, knocking for admission to the seats vacated in 1861. Then, and not till then, peace was proclaimed throughout the land, and authoritatively announced to all nations.

It is not correct that the President of the United

States made those State governments, or caused them to be made, by force or intimidation. The Union armies, of which he was commander-in-chief, lingered, indeed, in the rebel States, to keep the peace in the event of surprise during the transition from civil war. The popular action there was, nevertheless, spontaneous, and the Executive confined itself to the form of suggestion and advice of which President Lincoln had already wisely set an accepted example. The new State constitutions were the best attainable at the time, without direct application of force. They were adequate to the emergency, and they were open, like all similar constitutions, to further revisions and improvement, with the lapse of time and the increase of popular knowledge and virtue in the several States.

Congress hesitated, debated, postponed. The rebel States were no longer in rebellion. They were not received into the Union. The people, North as well as South, were excited: new schemes were proposed, new party combinations formed. There was no longer the Union party, which had conducted the country through the fiercest civil war ever known. But that party was seen resolving itself, in an untimely hour, into ancient divisions, the Republican and Democratic parties. An advanced section of one party demanded new and farther guaranties, and entertained wild propositions of retaliation, confiscation, proscription, disfranchisement, and other penalties, as conditions of reconciliation. A reactionary section of the other insisted that all delays were not only hazardous, but that all conditions whatever were unnecessary, unreasonable, and unconstitutional. One party insisted that there could be no safe peace without immediately extending suffrage to the freedmen by means no matter how rash, unconstitutional, or violent. The other insisted that a proceeding so abrupt, so violent, so inconsistent with the provisions of the Constitution of the United States in regard to the conservation of the States rights and individual freedom would inevitably inaugurate a war of races. What did all this indicate but a controversy about the new constitutions to be formed in the southern States? What did imperial intervention in St. Domingo or Mexico mean, but a demand of such a constitution there as should be acceptable to France?

It is not my purpose to revive now, or even to retrace, that long and angry debate. We all see how it has resulted thus far. All the Representatives sent to Congress by the rebel States in 1865 have been rejected without regard to their qualifications or their loyalty. All the loyal State governments formed in 1865 have been abrogated, without regard to their loyalty, with the exercise of military force. Subaltern army officers have been placed by Congress in charge of the several States. Congress has enfranchised and has disfranchised in those States, just as seemed best calculated to secure the acceptance of constitutions prescribed by itself through military agents in communities where no rebel force has been seen for nearly four years. The President, with a tenacity that has provoked the scrutiny of the nation and challenged the judgment of mankind, has held fast to two things, namely, the wise and humane plan of his predecessor, and, what is infinitely more important, the Constitution of the United States, just as he found both. For this adherence he has been brought to trial on impeachment in constitutional form, for pretended high crimes and misdemeanors, and duly acquitted. The nation has thus been called on to sustain the new shock of political assassination of its chosen and beloved head, and to encounter afterwards the wild and reckless proceedings of inconsiderate leaders, such as kept Mexico in a condition of anarchy through a period of forty years, and which have left hardly one stable or even peaceful republic remaining in South America. Most of the States organized in this irregular manner have sent their Representatives to Congress, and those Representatives have been admitted, while all the State governments through whose machinery those Representatives were sent, or nearly all, are invoking the Congress of the United States to suspend the writ of *habeas corpus*, to establish martial law, to assume and to confide to military agents the entire business of government in those States, under alarms and fears of renewed insurrection and restoration of slavery.

It is not my purpose to vindicate or even to explain the part I myself have had in these transactions and debates, instructive as I am sure they will prove to future ages. I simply say that as I stood firmly by the wise and magnanimous policy of President Lincoln in his life, so I have adhered to the same policy since his mortal remains were committed to an untimely grave, and I have adhered with equal fidelity to his constitutional successor.

When the civil war came to an end, no wise man supposed that the transition could be abruptly made from a state of civil war to a condition of tranquillity and peace without occasional disturbance to be produced by inconsiderate individuals, and even by unlawful combinations of disappointed and excited men. On the contrary, every wise man knew that reconciliation, however hindered, could not be long deferred, and that constituent States of this Union, no matter how far they had wandered from the ways of loyalty, must sooner or later be again received into the Union. I have habitually thought that all needful political wisdom in regard to that crisis was contained in the scriptural injunction, "agree with your adversary quickly," and that this injunction, which is true in regard to all adversaries, is especially true when your adversaries are estranged brethren.

So much, my friends, for the past. What now is the present situation? We have heard for three years alarms of premature reconciliation, the advantages of procrastination, the dangers of reaction and renewed rebellion. At last the cry is frantically uttered by all parties, "*Peace,* peace!" "Let us have *peace!*" [loud applause,] when there is no peace in the sense implied, but only forebodings of renewed war. What does the country need in view of this painful situation? I answer my own question. It needs just what it needed in 1865—the admission of loyal Representatives from the late rebel States into the Congress of the United States; and it needs at this time and at our hands no more. When you have given to the southern States the places in Congress where they will have a constitutional hearing, the people there will acquiesce in what Congress may require, and their mouths will be closed on all constitutional topics that have produced agitation and excitement. The States which send those Representatives must have loyal representative governments to determine who, what party, what interest, or what faction shall enjoy the power or discharge the responsibilities of government there. We must indeed keep the peace for them, if they cannot keep it themselves. We must, therefore, support and maintain existing governments there to that end ; but it belongs to the people of those States, just as much as it belongs to the people of this State, to say whether they shall live under one form of loyal republican government or another, and under one administration of loyal republican government or under another. I do not ask or require that representatives or governments there shall be white, or black, or mixed. I insist only that they shall be representative men, freely chosen in those States by the people themselves, and not by outside compulsion or dictation. I do, indeed, know that the best form of republican government existing in any of the States is capable of amendment, as I am sure that it will hereafter be greatly amended. Being no conservative, in the narrow meaning of that word, I not only do not oppose, but I favor all such amendments, and accept but one limitation for my efforts in that direction. That limitation is the Constitution of the United States; which enjoins non-intervention upon me, so long as those States are loyal to the Union, and keep the public peace, their own peace, and the peace of the Union. I shall not, therefore, take the sword into my own hand; or put it in the hand of any other person, to effect a reform by force in those States, which, I am sure, will be effected much sooner and much more permanently through the exercise of persuasion and reason. As little do I think it my duty to use the sword to cut away and remove what has already been done in those States, [applause,] whether it was necessarily done or unnecessarily and unwisely done. As I thought the situation which existed in 1865 ought to be accepted by a reasonable, patriotic, and humane administration, so do I think now the situation which exists in 1868, after the best efforts have been made to secure a better, ought to be accepted.

I am not without hope, my friends, that this painful national dilemma may be solved before the end of the present administration, as all our other national difficulties have been or will be. The ambitions of parties and chiefs must come to a rest with the close of this election, and calmness and tranquillity must sooner or later resume their sway over the public mind. In that case, I shall have little desire to speak concerning the future administration of the Government, content to have performed with singleness of purpose, and with all my ability, my duties under the administration with which I am personally connected. It is, on the other hand, possible that the dilemma of reconciliation may continue unsolved, and may require the attention of the new administration. It is in this respect that I deem the present choice of a future Chief Magistrate not merely important, but perhaps critically so, as the last two choices were. One consideration alone is sufficient to determine my judgment in this emergency. I cannot forget that the civil war has closed with two great political achievements: the one the saving of the integrity of the Union, the other the abolition of African slavery. Personally, I see no cause to fear, in any case, a reaction in which both or either of these great national attainments can be lost. They are in harmony with the spirit of the age and the established progress of mankind.

My confidence, however, in this respect, is not indulged, nor do I expect it to be entertained by all, nor even by the majority of my patriotic fellow-citizens, who were engaged with me in making or aiding those great achievements. Their wounds, unlike my own, are yet unhealed ; their sacrifices, unlike my own, are yet unrewarded. They have been, therefore, and they will continue to be, apprehensive in that regard, and those apprehensions will increase with every indiscreet proceeding, or even utterance, of any person or parties who were ever compromised in, or who ever sympathized with, the rebellion or with African slavery. Confidence is, in the case of most men, though it is not in mine, a plant of slow growth. Not only is it true that such apprehensions, however unreasonable they may be, cannot be safely disregarded, but it is equally true that they are to be respected and indulged, because of the moral influence they will exert in favor of union, freedom, and progress in all future times and throughout the world. The magistrates who are to preside, then, in the work of reconciliation hereafter, ought, like those who have preceded in former stages of that work, to be men drawn from and representing that class of citizens who maintained the Government in the prosecution of the civil war and in the abolition of slavery. [Great applause.] In no other hands could the work of reconciliation be expected to be successful, because of a different sort of magistrates would be profoundly and generally suspected a willingness to betray the transcendent public interests which were gained and secured by the war.

The attitude of each of the political parties in this canvass is, in some respects, different from what I myself could have desired or would have advised. Very great wrongs have been committed in the name of liberty by the Republicans of the United Stats, as great crimes were committed in the same holy name by French republicans in the revolution of 1789. Nevertheless, the Republican party neither rests under any suspicion of its devotion to human freedom, nor can it fall under any such suspicion.

The Democratic party, I do not now propose to say with how much justice, has not so conducted itself in its corporate and responsible action as to secure the entire confidence of a loyal and exacting people in its unconditional and uncompromising adherence to the Union, or in its acceptance and approval of the effective abolition of slavery. I entertain no jealousy of the Democratic party or its leaders, and no unfriendly or uncharitable feelings towards that great constituency. On the other hand, I cherish a grateful appreciation of the patriotism, the magnanimity, the heroism of many of my fellow-citizens with whom I have cheerfully labored and co-operated, while they still retained their adhesion to the Democratic party. How could I distrust the loyalty or the virtue of Andrew Johnson, of General Hancock, General McClellan. Senator Buckalew of Pennsylvania, of Senator Hendricks of Indiana, or his associate, Mr. Niblack, or of Mr. Cox of Ohio, to whom, personally, more than any other member, is due the passage of the constitutional amendment in Congress abolishing African slavery. I have, therefore, regarded with sincere, and, I trust, patriotic satisfaction, the efforts of Democratic leaders, as well those made in 1864 at Chicago, as the greater ones made in New York in 1868, to lift the Democratic party up to a plane, upon attaining which all the errors and short-comings of any of its members during the civil war would at once drop off from the Democratic party's back, as the burden of Christian fell off his back when he "came up to the cross."

If the Democratic party had only reached that plane I should have felt that further concern on my part about the work of reconciliation might be dismissed. In that case we should have had the two great parties of the country substantially agreed in the right, just as the two great parties of the country, in my judgment, in 1852 agreed in the wrong. In 1852 both parties agreed in the compromise of 1850, which accepted the fugitive slave law, allowed the extension of African slavery, and prohibited discussion upon it in the National Congress forever. If the Democratic party in 1868 had lifted themselves to the position I have supposed, we should then have had both parties of the country practically agreeing in the justice, wisdom, and humanity of the Government in the civil war, and of the abolition of slavery; and at the same time agreeing upon the ripeness of the time and the necessity for peace and fraternal affection. The Democratic party having failed to do so, its preparation to assume the responsibilities of a rescued and regenerated nation must be delayed four years. To confide those responsibilities to that party in its present position would be to continue, perhaps increase, the lamentable political excitement which alone has prevented the complete restoration of the Union to the present time.

I well know that it will be said, on the other hand, with much show of reason, that extreme idealists and agitators may be expected to exert a dangerous influence under a new Republican administration, by reason of their having gathered themselves into the ranks of the supporters of the Republican candidate. This, however, is no new dilemma for me, or for many of you, my old friends. We were required year after year to support Henry Clay as the best of two choices, although he disavowed all that time the noble principles which we held concerning the irrepressible conflict between freedom and slavery. We did so wisely. We were required in 1852 to support General Scott as the best of two candidates offered us, although he was put upon a platform which maintained the fugitive slave law, and declared it perpetually inviolable. We wisely did that. No one citizen may ever hope to find a candidate perfectly acceptable to himself, and yet find that the grounds of his own choice for that candidate are accepted by all his fellow-citizens who concur with him in that preference. No one can foresee six months beforehand what the political exigencies of the country may be, or how the administration of the Government must act when they occur. In 1860 we elected a President simply to maintain the cause of freedom against legislative aggression. That administration encountered no such difficulty. The danger apprehended had passed away before that administration came into power, and it found itself confronted, instead of that danger, by a rebellion which taxed all its energies, and opened a conflict which resulted in the immediate abolition of slavery; an event which had not been before expected to occur in less than fifty years! So I think none can now foresee the especial line of official duty which a new administration may find it necessary to pursue.

We are impatient of the slow progress we make towards great national ends. We often magnify the obstacles we meet and deem them insurmountable; but time is always busy in abating those difficulties and smoothing our way. The result of the election, if favorable to the candidates of our choice, will put an end to all the debates which it has excited, and prepare the popular mind to accept now what it has heretofore rejected, namely, the most practicable and easy solution of the national embarrassments. In any case I console myself with the reflection that as wisdom was not born with the administration of Abraham Lincoln, so it will not die with the administration of Andrew Johnson.

I have not entertained you on this occasion, my friends, with eulogiums upon your candidates or any of them; or with aspersions of the candidates of your opponents or any of them. I need scarcely remind you that I have no such habit. Certainly there is no occasion now for that line of debate. All those candidates are well known, more widely known indeed than any candidates who have ever before been named for the high offices for which they are designated, since the first administration of the Government. They are better known, because they are historically identified with national trials of surpassing magnitude, and of deep interest to all mankind.

It remains only now to thank you for your indulgence. If I have come among you late, I have, nevertheless, come in time. I have neither questioned the opinions nor the motives which have governed your civil conduct since we last met. I have troubled you with no explanations of my own. We have come together again at a time when I am approaching the end of a service in the executive department of our Government as long as has ever been vouchsafed by this nation to any citizen in the Department which I have conducted. Practically, I am already returned among you a private citizen, as I was when I was called into that service. The responsibilities and trials which have attended the Government during that period have transcended in dignity and in interest any through which our Government had previously passed, except, perhaps, in the Revolution. I trust that no equal responsibilities or trials are in reserve for the next administration, or are to be encountered by any future administration for many generations to come. I am by no means confident that I have not often erred. I have, nevertheless, a humble trust that at least these things can be said of me, by those of you whose friendship I am still permitted to enjoy, namely, that no act or word of mine brought on or hastened the lamentable civil war whose wounds it is our present object to heal. But, on the contrary, no act that I could perform, nor any word that I could utter, to prevent or even delay that calamity, was withheld. When that civil war came and found me on the ramparts of the Constitution, and so long as it was waged, no act or word of mine encouraged an enemy of the United States, at home or abroad; while, on the contrary, every act that I could lawfully perform, and every word that I could lawfully utter to save the national life, fearfully exposed at home and abroad, was performed and spoken. No act or word of mine has consented to the prolongation of slavery a single day. On the contrary, my hand and seal is found upon the one international act which remained to abolish the African slave-trade throughout the world, and on the military proclamation and the constitutional amendment, that forever abolished slavery itself in the United States. [Applause.]

No one State in the Union, nor any fraction of a State, was, by any action or word of mine, driven or allowed to separate itself from the Union. On the contrary, every act or word that I could lawfully perform or speak to prevent that wild treason or madness was spoken with all the decision, and yet with all the moderation, that such counsels required. When that frightful rebellion ceased, no one State of the Union, or fraction of a State, was, by any action or word of mine, repelled from returning to its allegiance. On the contrary, every act or word of mine that was useful, or that promised to be useful, in bringing those revolutionary States back to reinforce and reinvigorate the Union which they had so rashly attempted to destroy, was seasonably performed and spoken. No seat in Congress constitutionally assigned to any State or community within the United States is now, or ever has been, one moment kept vacant or unoccupied through any prohibition, obstruction, or hindrance of mine, by word or deed. On the contrary, the crime, and only crime, of which I now know that I am impeached, is that of being too precipitate in the policy of national reconciliation and peace. No State, nor any citizen, by any act or word of mine, has suffered disfranchisement or confiscation, nor, except for the assassination of Abraham Lincoln, has any one endured penalties or punishment. Throughout my life an advocate of universal suffrage for the exile and the emigrant, and even the slave, I give to those classes the support and patronage which the Constitution of my country permits and allows. [Applause.] No injury, insult, or other offence has been committed against our country, or any one of its citizens, by any foreign State or nation, without having found me employing all the constitutional power confided to me, with all the ability I possessed, to redress the wrong. The prestige of the nation I humbly trust has not been lost or impaired. I almost dare to think it has been elevated amid all the domestic trials of civil war and factions. The Monroe doctrine, which eight years ago was merely a theory, is now an irreversible fact. Certainly the country is not less now, but is larger than I found it when I entered my last public service. It has already begun to enjoy the wealth of the polar seas, and I am sure it is not my fault if its flag is still jealously excluded by European nations from the ever-verdant islands of the Carribean sea. When I left you to enter the public service, insurrectionary armies were being gathered into the field of domestic war, and the hollowness of national friendships was experienced in the melancholy fact that the United States had not one assured and sympathizing friend in the world except the republic of Switzerland. It is a source of satisfaction to us all that our country has now many new and established friends amongst the nations, while for myself I am sure, as I trust you will soon be for yourselves, that they have no longer any dangerous domestic foe within their borders. If now I shall find the ancient cheer which heretofore presided at your firesides in winter; if I shall find the birds still lingering in your gardens and groves as in the olden time in the summer; if the trout are not exhausted in your brooks, or the perch in your lakes; if industry still dwells in your shops and you still want new shops and houses to be built for your mechanics and laborers; if piety shall prevail as heretofore in your churches, and charity toward each other, and humanity toward all conditions of men shall distinguish your political assemblies, then indeed we are about to renew, with mutual satisfaction, an acquaintance which, while it existed unbroken, was happy for us all, and which for me has been too long and painfully suspended. [Great applause.]

www.ingramcontent.com/pod-product-compliance
Lightning Source LLC
LaVergne TN
LVHW011121110826
845150LV00008B/2215

9781418196943